Contents

Chapter 1

MY LIP

Hi! I'm Red Rosie and I was born with a cleft lip.

I was the first born of my litter.

I was a fighter from the start!

I had to be because it was hard for

me to eat with a cleft lip.

I tried to get milk from my mama

like my brother and sister,

but it was not easy for me, not easy at all.

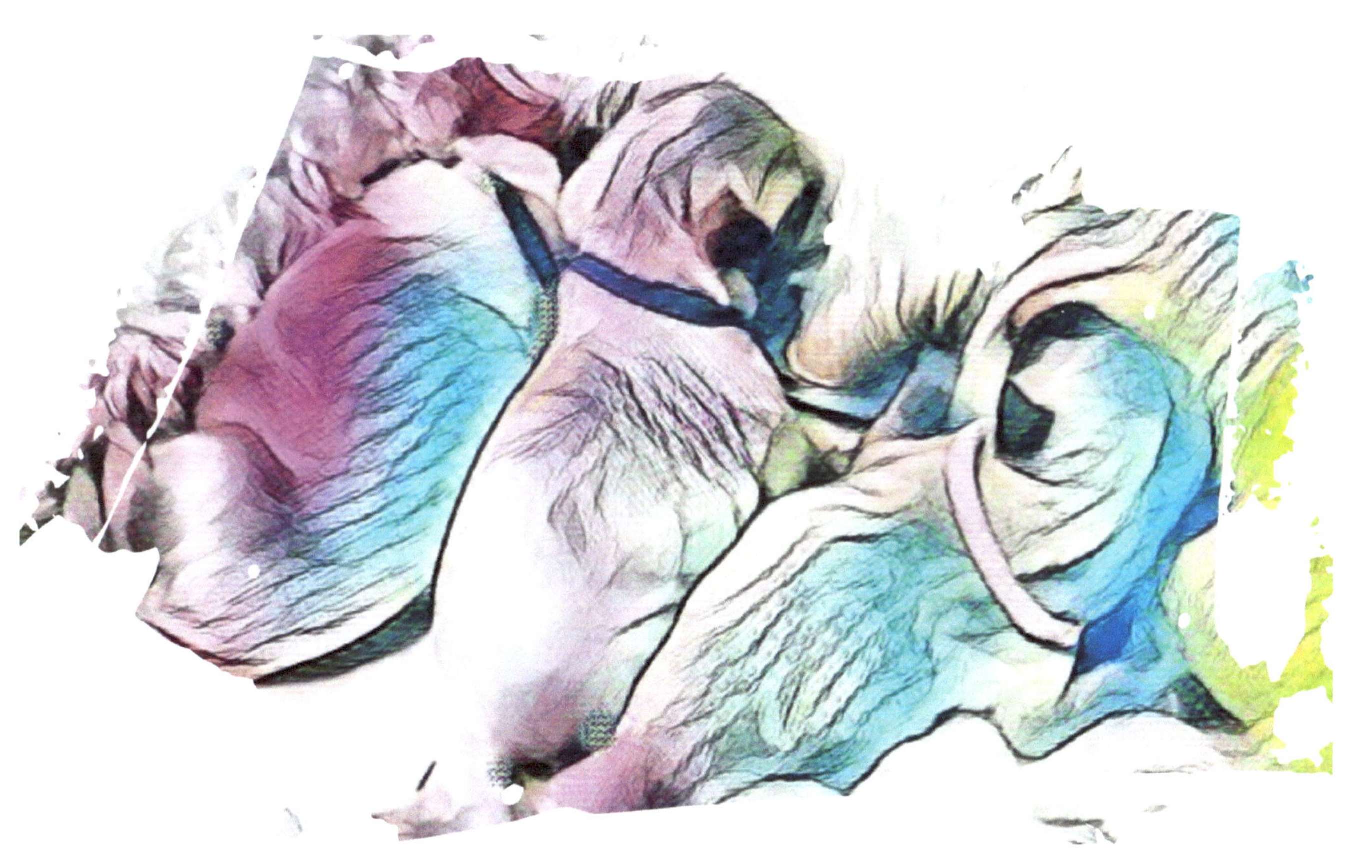

Chapter 2

MY MAMA

My mama was a good mama.

She always made sure the I was close to her.

She licked me a lot so that I would eat.

My brother could do it...

My sister could do it...

But I could not!!!

I was mad!

I was hungry!

I wanted milk tooooooooo!

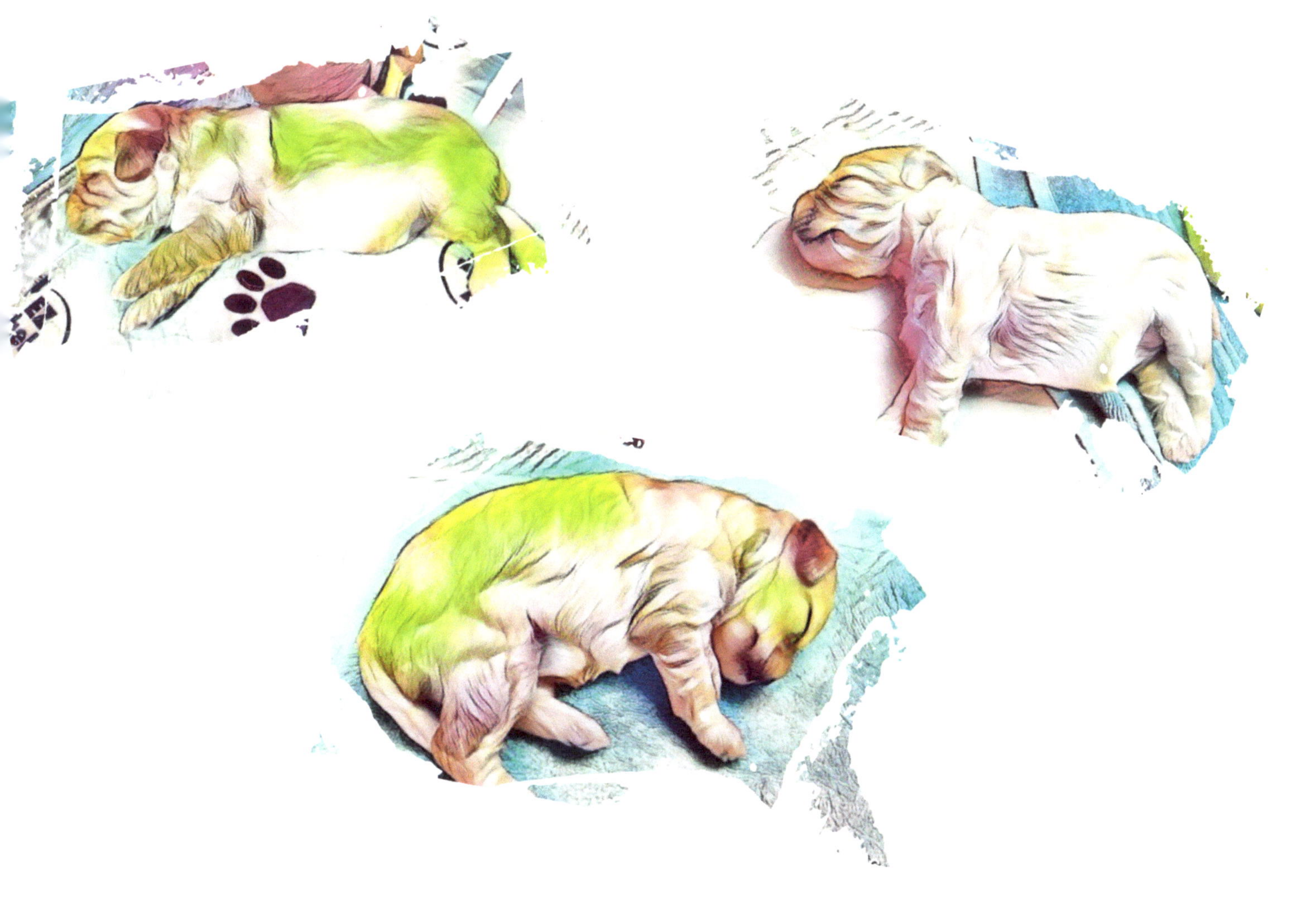

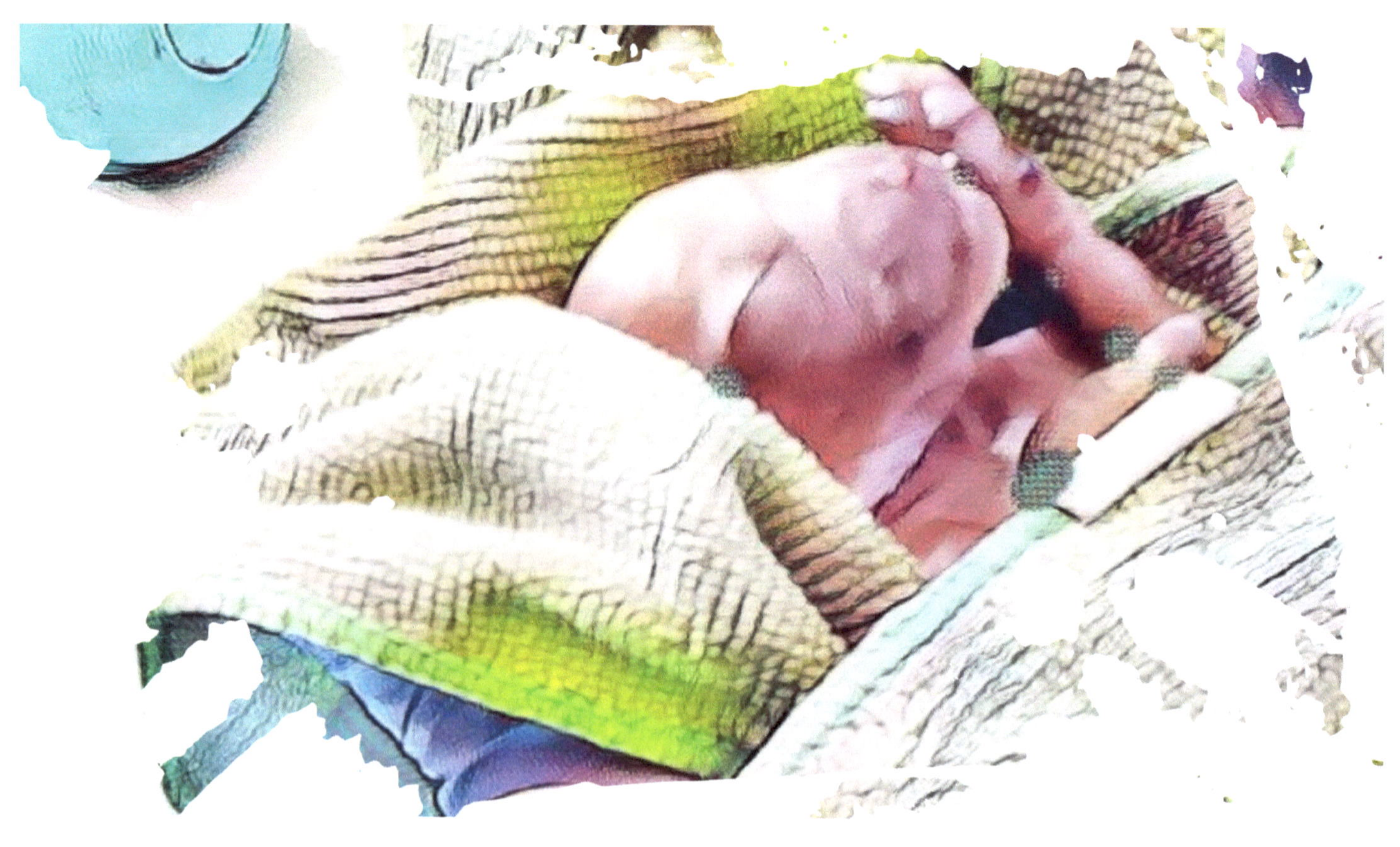

I pushed.

I pulled.

I pushed and I pulled, but it was no use.

I just couldn't drink enough milk.

I needed help fast.

Chapter 3
THE VETERINARIAN

A very nice lady took me to the veterinarian.

Everyone looked at my mouth.

No one was sure if I would be able to eat

on my own...ever!

The veterinarian said that my mouth was strong.

She said that I was determined.

She said that I was a fighter and that if someone could feed me with a feeding tube until I was able to lap my food from a bowl, I just might live.

I was strong, but I needed help.

I was determined, but I could not do it on my own.

I still fought to get milk from my mama,

but I couldn't get enough.

Was there anyone who would help me?

Yes!!

There was someone who would help me!!

My person, she fed me with a feeding tube, and she helped me to live!

But my lip wasn't my only problem...

Chapter 4

MY BROTHER SKIP

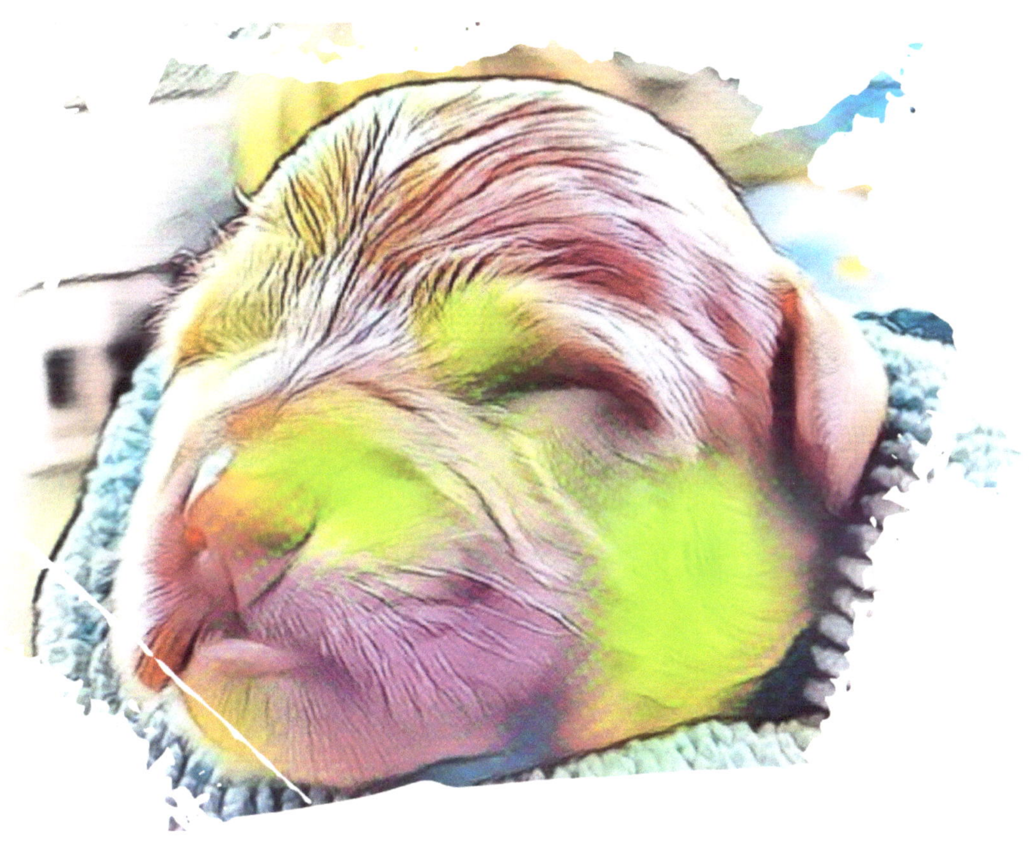

Soon my people realized that my mama didn't have enough milk for me, my brother and my sister.

My brother Skip drank most of it!

He drank and he drank, and he drank some more until there was nothing left for me!

Oh, I tried to push him off, yes, I did! I was not going to give up easily, but he was just too fast.

So, my people helped my mama. They gave her special food and a creamy pudding so that she could make more milk for all of us.

Soon we did have enough.

We were all very happy.

We were all very full.

We were all growing, but I grew the slowest.

Kilogram by kilogram I grew, but no one knew if there could be another problem, one that could not be seen as easily as my lip.

The people still feared that I might not live.

But they never gave up on me.

They kept feeding me.

They kept loving me.

They kept telling me not to give up.

I was not giving up!

I wanted to live!

I wanted to eat!

I wanted to grow into a playful puppy!!

Chapter 5
GOODBYE FEEDING TUBE

When I was three weeks old,

I saw my first bowl of milk.

It was special milk for puppies.

It smelled DELICIOUS.

Do you know what I did?

I lapped!

I lapped and I lapped, and I lapped!

All the people were so happy that they cheered for me!

"Yay, Rosie!! Good girl!!," they said.

They hugged and kissed me when I was finished.

I did it! I ate on my own!

I didn't get any in my nose.

It all went down into my belly.

Now I had a chance, a big chance, thanks to the veterinarian who knew my mouth was strong, and to the people who loved and helped me.

This was the day that I said, "Goodbye," to my feeding tube.

It was a very good day.

Chapter 6
NOT ALONE

When I was born, the first thing I wanted to do, no, the first thing I needed to do was to eat.

I couldn't eat by myself, but I was not alone.

I had help.

I had a lot of help.

I couldn't speak for myself, but some very good people spoke up for me

Now, I am here to tell you something important.

You are not alone either!

When you need help with something that is hard to do by yourself, ask someone you trust to help you!

My name is Rosie, Red Rosie, and this is my birthday story.

Not Chapter 7

CONNECT WITH ROSIE

So, did you like my birthday story?

My story is true!

I was born in and live in Pennsylvania.

I have a lot of room to run and to play.

I love my family and my friends!

I'm happy that you read this book about me.

Your family can follow me on Instagram if you would like to see real photos and videos of me enjoying the life that my people helped to give me.

I'm a silly puppy having fun and spreading hope!